MAYER SMITH

The Billionaire's Secret Recipe Revealed

Contents

One

The Hidden Identity

The bright lights of the cooking competition stage flickered, casting sharp shadows over the stainless-steel countertops. The air smelled of fresh herbs, simmering sauces, and the distinct hum of anticipation. The audience, a sea of eager faces in the studio, seemed to blur into one giant blur of excitement. Somewhere among them, hidden beneath the carefully constructed facade, was a woman who had everything, yet nothing.

Victoria Reynolds stood at the far end of the stage, pretending to inspect the sharpness of a chef's knife as her eyes swept over the bustling set. The cameras captured every movement, the boom microphones hovering just above her head, recording every breath and every stir. She was a master of deception, and she had to be.

Dressed in a simple, yet practical, chef's coat, her hair tied neatly in a messy bun, Victoria looked every bit like the kind of contestant who could disappear into the background. She was an unknown, a mystery to the audience, the judges, and most importantly, the other contestants. Her true identity was carefully guarded—no one here knew she was the billionaire heiress behind the most successful food empire in the world. The empire that had once been her father's legacy, now hers to control. The empire that made her a household name in the culinary world, though her face had never graced a public appearance.

But here, on this stage, none of that mattered. No one knew that behind the crisp white apron she wore, there was a woman who had everything—money, power, influence, and an empire at her fingertips. The reality of that life, however, had been hollow for too long. Victoria had learned over the years that her name, her wealth, and her connections had isolated her. People weren't interested in her; they were interested in the business she could provide. The last thing she wanted was for anyone to recognize her as the queen of the food world.

And so, here she was, standing in the middle of a nationally televised cooking competition, disguised as a contestant like everyone else. She had entered under the name "Vera Lee," a fabricated persona born out of necessity. Her goal wasn't to win the competition; no, she was here for something far more personal—something more valuable than any prize money or recognition. She was here to prove to herself that she could be more than just a brand.

She could already hear the voices of the contestants around her, their low murmurs of nervous excitement filling the air. Some were seasoned professionals, others were amateurs hoping for their big break. But all of them, like her, wanted validation. Validation that they were worthy of being here.

And then, like a whirlwind, the host's voice boomed from the loudspeakers, cutting through the noise and commanding the room's attention.

"Welcome, everyone, to the most anticipated cooking competition of the year! Our contestants today will face off in a series of challenges that will test their skill, creativity, and ability to stand under pressure. One of them will walk away with the title of 'The Ultimate Chef' and a career-defining opportunity. But only one can claim that prize. So, let the competition begin!"

Victoria's fingers tightened around the knife handle as the camera swung to her, and she instinctively straightened her posture. The last thing she wanted was to draw attention to herself, but the bright lens zooming in on her face made it impossible to blend in. Her eyes shifted down, staring at the polished countertop, willing herself not to be visible.

But then she felt it—the presence of someone standing right beside her. She could sense the sharpness in the air, the heat of another person's gaze upon her. She slowly turned her head and found herself face-to-face with him—the celebrity chef everyone had been talking about for months. He was tall, confident, and every inch the media sensation he was, his broad shoulders encased in a fitted black chef's jacket. His signature smirk was already on display, that same smirk she had seen on television countless times.

"Looks like we're neighbors," he said, his voice low and teasing, with an edge of arrogance that she had come to expect from a man of his stature.

Victoria stiffened, catching herself before the words slipped out. She had been trying to avoid him, but there he was, standing within arm's reach, watching her with eyes that could read the faintest of shifts in her body language.

"I suppose so," she replied, keeping her tone light and indifferent. She needed to play it cool. He didn't know her, and that was how it had to stay.

The chef raised an eyebrow, his eyes scanning the counter where her hands were now carefully arranging the ingredients in front of her. "I have to say, you've got a nice setup there. What are you cooking?"

Victoria smiled politely, her fingers brushing over the ripe tomatoes she had selected earlier. "I'm thinking of a simple, rustic dish. Something hearty but elegant."

He smirked again, clearly not impressed. "Simple, huh? You'll need more than that to stand out in this competition."

She caught the subtle challenge in his tone, the spark of competition dancing in his eyes. It was obvious he didn't believe in underestimating anyone, but he had no idea who he was really speaking to. He didn't know that her simple dish was going to blow the judges away.

"Maybe," she said, keeping her voice steady. "But sometimes, the simplest things are the most memorable."

Before he could respond, the host called the contestants to attention, announcing the start of the first challenge. The celebrity chef turned away from her with a small nod, as though acknowledging her presence for the first time. Victoria's breath caught as she took her first step into the heat of the competition.

The challenge itself was straightforward: create a dish using only five mystery ingredients that would surprise the judges. But what really concerned Victoria was the chef's ability to challenge her in ways she hadn't expected. He was no ordinary culinary expert; he had a reputation for pushing contestants to their limits, breaking them down before building them back up into better versions of themselves.

Victoria wasn't sure whether she was ready for that kind of transformation, but she had no choice. Her whole life had been spent hiding behind the walls of her empire, where nothing was ever real. But here, on this stage, she was forced to confront the truth of her own cooking—of her own abilities.

As the clock started, she tossed the first few ingredients into the pan, expertly seasoning the dish as her hands moved with precision. But even as she worked, she couldn't shake the feeling of eyes on her. The celebrity chef's gaze had not left her, and it was clear that he was scrutinizing every move she made.

Her heart beat faster with each passing second, but she refused to be intimidated. She wasn't just cooking for the judges. She wasn't just cooking to win. No, this was her chance to prove to herself that she could do something with her hands that no amount of money could buy—something real.

As she plated the dish and prepared to present it to the judges, Victoria felt a strange calm settle over her. She had done everything she could. Now, she just had to wait for the verdict. Would they see through her disguise? Would they guess who she really was?

But more importantly, would she be able to resist the urge to reveal herself to the man who had unwittingly made her question everything she thought she knew about herself?

The moment she set the plate in front of the judges, she realized one thing—this was only the beginning. The game had just started.

Two

The Celebrity Chef

The tension in the kitchen was palpable, a suffocating pressure that seemed to settle into the very air. The clock on the wall ticked relentlessly down, a constant reminder of how little time they had. Contestants scrambled to pull together their dishes, some working with fierce concentration, while others wore anxious expressions, their movements uncertain. Victoria's heart was beating a little faster than normal, but she refused to show it. She couldn't afford to. Not here, not now.

Her focus remained on the dish in front of her, a carefully constructed balance of textures and flavors. She had worked countless hours in her private kitchens perfecting her skills, but this—this was different. This was the real world, a world where every minute counted, every decision was scrutinized. There was no hiding behind the walls of her empire now. It was just her, her ingredients, and the looming presence of the celebrity chef.

The thought of him sent a ripple of unease through her. His piercing eyes, his cocky demeanor, his reputation as a kitchen tyrant—he was everything Victoria had avoided in the public eye. She had built her food empire through years of hard work and innovation, not by being in the spotlight. The public didn't know her as a chef; they knew her as a businesswoman, the heiress to a multi-billion-dollar empire. But here, on this stage, in this competition, she had to prove herself as just another contestant. Her identity as Victoria Reynolds was irrelevant. She was simply Vera Lee now—a nobody, a mystery.

And yet, there he was, the man everyone feared and admired in equal measure—the celebrity chef who had brought his own brand of chaos to this competition. She had seen him on television, his sharp critiques and no-nonsense approach to cooking, turning even the most seasoned chefs into quivering wrecks. But it wasn't just his reputation that unsettled her. It was the way he had looked at her earlier, with a knowing gaze that made her feel both seen and invisible at the same time.

Victoria took a deep breath and refocused. The time for distractions had passed. The celebrity chef would be watching closely, but she had a plan. Her goal was not to stand out, not to prove to the world who she was. It was to finish this competition without revealing herself—without him uncovering the truth.

The first round of the competition was nearly over, and the contestants were lining up their plates. The celebrity chef, standing tall with his arms crossed and an air of quiet authority, moved through the kitchen like a lion surveying his domain. His every movement seemed deliberate, each step calculated. He wasn't just any judge—he was a force of nature, and no one in this room, least of all Victoria, would be able to escape his scrutiny.

The host called out the contestants' names one by one, their plates presented to the panel of judges. Victoria's pulse quickened as her turn drew near. As the last contestant in line, she had no choice but to watch as one by one, the others presented their creations. Some dishes were met with approval, others with sharp critiques. The celebrity chef offered little more than a nod of acknowledgment or a raised eyebrow, but his words were cutting when he spoke.

Finally, it was her turn.

"Vera Lee," the host called, and the spotlight shifted onto her. Victoria stood tall, trying to mask the tightening in her chest. She could hear the hushed murmurs of the audience, but she didn't let them distract her. She had to remain calm. She had to remain in control.

She carefully plated her dish, a dish that was simple in its ingredients but layered in its flavors—a humble bowl of roasted vegetables with a rich, earthy sauce. It was a dish that spoke to her roots, to the times when she first fell in love with cooking. It wasn't flashy or extravagant. It didn't scream for attention. But it was honest. And she hoped it would be enough.

She approached the judges' table, her heart pounding. The celebrity chef was seated in the center, his sharp eyes trained on her every move. He didn't smile. He didn't need to. His presence alone was enough to make her feel exposed.

Victoria set the plate down gently, keeping her eyes on the dish. She couldn't bring herself to look at him—not yet. She knew the eyes of the judges were on her, but it was the chef's gaze she dreaded most. She couldn't let him see through her, not when everything hinged on this one moment.

The celebrity chef took a moment before speaking. His eyes never left the plate in front of him, his lips pressed into a thin line as he examined the dish.

"Simple," he muttered under his breath, just loud enough for everyone to hear. The word cut through the room like a knife.

Victoria's stomach twisted, but she kept her face neutral. She had anticipated this. She had prepared for the critique.

"Tell me, Vera," the celebrity chef continued, his voice smooth, controlled. "What makes this dish stand out from the others?"

She could feel the weight of the room on her shoulders as every contestant turned their attention to her. Her heart skipped a beat, but she didn't falter. She took a steady breath and responded.

"It's not about standing out," she said softly. "It's about understanding the ingredients—knowing their story, their origin.

Roasting these vegetables brings out their natural sweetness, and the sauce? It's a balance of textures. It's simple, but it's honest."

The celebrity chef's eyes flickered briefly to her, his expression unreadable. He wasn't moved. But then, he didn't need to be. He had heard similar lines from countless contestants over the years.

"You think honesty is enough?" he asked, his tone laced with challenge.

Victoria didn't answer immediately. Instead, she met his gaze. The fire in his eyes was unmistakable—he wasn't just a chef. He was a man who lived and breathed competition, who thrived on pushing others to their breaking points. He wasn't just testing her cooking skills. He was testing her.

She swallowed the lump in her throat. "Sometimes, it is," she replied quietly.

A long silence followed as the judges sampled the dish. The celebrity chef remained silent, his expression impossible to read. He placed his fork down and turned his attention to her once more.

"I think you've missed the mark, Vera," he said, his voice devoid of warmth. "This dish lacks the spark I was hoping to see. It's safe. Too safe."

Victoria's heart dropped, but she didn't allow herself to react.

"But there's potential," he added, his tone shifting slightly. "You've got the technical skill. Now show me the passion. Show me the heart."

Those words hung in the air, and for a moment, it felt as though everything had shifted. For the first time in the competition, the celebrity chef was looking at her—not as a contestant, but as something more. His eyes lingered on her, and Victoria could feel the weight of his scrutiny.

The other judges murmured their agreement, and as they turned their attention to the next contestant, Victoria felt the sting of the chef's words. Safe. Too safe.

She had expected harsh critiques, but she hadn't expected this. She hadn't expected him to see through her so quickly. It was only the beginning, and already, the competition was becoming far more personal than she had ever anticipated.

As she turned and walked back to her station, Victoria couldn't shake the feeling that the celebrity chef wasn't just testing her cooking. He was testing her resolve. And she wasn't sure how much longer she could hide behind her disguise.

The game was on, and there was no turning back now.

Three

The First Challenge

The kitchen buzzed with frantic energy, each contestant trying to keep pace with the ticking clock. The constant clatter of pots and pans echoed against the stainless steel walls, the hiss of hot oil in the fryers, the sharp scent of garlic and onions filling the air. Victoria stood at her station, her hands steady as she measured out her ingredients. The competition had intensified in a way she hadn't expected, and every second now felt like a race against time. There was no room for error.

Her mind raced with thoughts of the previous challenge, the harsh critique from the celebrity chef still lingering in her chest. The sting of his words had settled deep into her, but she refused to let it define her. This competition was no longer just about the dish. It was about something far more personal.

She couldn't afford to falter. Not now.

The host's voice cut through the chaos, announcing the rules for the first real challenge of the competition. "Contestants, for today's challenge, you will be preparing a three-course meal using only the ingredients provided in your baskets. You have one hour to prepare and present your dishes. The judges will be assessing you on creativity, technique, and, most importantly, how well you can elevate basic ingredients into something extraordinary."

Victoria's eyes flickered to the small basket of ingredients placed in front of her. Inside, she found a selection of vegetables— carrots, potatoes, and leeks—along with a small piece of fish and a few herbs. It wasn't much, and she could already hear the collective groans of disappointment from the other contestants. There was nothing fancy about these ingredients. No truffles, no exotic spices. Just simple, humble food.

But for Victoria, this was her moment. She wasn't intimidated by the challenge; in fact, it was exactly what she had hoped for. The true test wasn't in the luxury of ingredients but in the ability to transform the ordinary into the extraordinary. She had done it for years in the kitchens of her empire, taking raw, simple ingredients and turning them into something that could change the way people thought about food.

She glanced over to her left and saw the celebrity chef watching her from his station. His eyes were intense, scanning her every movement, his arms folded across his chest. Victoria could feel the weight of his gaze on her, but she refused to acknowledge it. If she could keep her focus, if she could push past the nerves that had surfaced when he criticized her dish earlier, then she could do this.

"Thirty minutes remaining!" the host's voice boomed, and the room seemed to exhale collectively. Victoria was no stranger to pressure. She had built a food empire from the ground up, managing kitchens, overseeing menus, and making decisions that impacted millions of dollars. But here, in front of the cameras, with the celebrity chef's eyes on her, it felt different.

She pushed the unease aside and focused on the task at hand. She reached for the fish, inspecting it carefully. It wasn't the best quality, but it would do. She decided to make a delicate fish dish with a vegetable puree, adding a twist with the herbs to create a contrast of flavors. The simplicity of the ingredients allowed her to showcase the depth of her technique. She could make this work.

Her knife sliced through the fish with precision, the blade moving in practiced strokes. As she worked, she couldn't help but notice how quiet the kitchen had become. The other contestants were all working furiously, but no one was speaking. The pressure of the challenge had settled on everyone, and Victoria could feel the tension in the air.

She glanced once more at the celebrity chef, who was watching her closely. His expression was unreadable, but she could see the slight furrow in his brow. He hadn't said anything yet, but she knew he was assessing her. She could practically feel his mind ticking over as he observed every movement.

Victoria had grown up with that kind of scrutiny—her father's harsh judgment, her family's expectations of perfection—but there was something about the celebrity chef's gaze that made her uneasy. It was more than just a critique of her cooking; it felt like a challenge to her very being. He wasn't just watching her food. He was watching her.

The clock ticked on, and Victoria worked faster. She sautéed the leeks with a splash of oil, the sizzling sound of the vegetables filling the space around her. Her hands moved fluidly, her mind sharp, but the ever-present pressure of the chef's eyes kept her on edge. She had to prove herself, not just as a cook, but as a person. There was something at stake here, something bigger than just winning a competition.

A shout rang out from one of the contestants, a young woman who had accidentally dropped her knife. It clattered to the floor, and the sudden noise broke Victoria's concentration. She watched as the young woman bent down to pick it up, her face flushed with embarrassment. Victoria could almost hear the inner voice that was telling her she wasn't good enough, that this was too much for her to handle.

But Victoria refused to be distracted. She couldn't afford to let anything derail her. Not now.

"Ten minutes left!" the host called out, and Victoria's heart skipped a beat. She had only ten minutes to finish the final touches on her dishes. The pressure was mounting, but she pushed herself harder.

She plated the fish delicately, garnishing it with the vegetable puree and a light drizzle of oil. It was simple, but it was elegant. She stepped back and surveyed the dish, knowing it wasn't perfect, but it was the best she could do given the circumstances. She glanced over at the celebrity chef, who was still watching her, his arms crossed. She had no idea what he was thinking, but she wasn't going to let his judgment stop her.

As she placed the dish in front of the judges, the room fell silent. The celebrity chef's eyes flickered to her, and for a moment, it felt as though the world had paused. His gaze was intense, but there was something else there too—something she couldn't quite place. Respect? Skepticism? She couldn't tell.

The judges began to taste the dishes, their faces inscrutable as they took their first bites. Victoria stood back, her hands trembling slightly as she watched. The pressure of the moment hung over her, but she refused to let it show. She had given her all in this dish. Now, all she could do was wait.

The celebrity chef took a bite of her dish, his face unreadable. His eyes never left her, but there was no sign of approval, no sign of critique. The seconds dragged on like hours. She couldn't read him, couldn't tell whether he was impressed or disappointed.

Finally, the silence was broken.

"Well, Vera," the celebrity chef said, his voice low, but with an edge of something else. "It's a good dish. Simple, but well executed. You've managed to make something from nothing.

But…"

Victoria's heart clenched. She knew that "but" was coming. She braced herself.

"But there's something missing," he continued, his eyes narrowing slightly. "It lacks the innovation, the spark that's required to set it apart. You have the skill, but you're holding back."

Victoria clenched her jaw, her hands balling into fists at her sides. He was right, in a way. She had played it safe. But there was more to this than just cooking. There was a reason she had held back. A reason she couldn't afford to let herself go all in.

She didn't respond. She just nodded, accepting the critique. She had expected this. She had always expected this from him.

The other judges offered their thoughts, but Victoria tuned them out, her mind spinning. The celebrity chef's words had cut deep, but they also solidified something inside her. She wasn't just playing to win this competition. She was playing to survive it.

As the round ended and the contestants returned to their stations, Victoria's mind raced. She had proven herself to some extent, but she knew it wasn't enough. She was still a step behind. And the celebrity chef had seen through her. He wasn't just looking for a winner; he was looking for someone who could push the boundaries.

And as much as she wanted to resist it, she knew he would be the one who would push her to her breaking point.

Four

Behind the Mask

The evening had drawn in, the lights above the kitchen studio now casting harsh shadows over the rows of stainless-steel countertops. The hum of the cameras, the soft murmur of the crew, and the clinking of utensils filled the space, all blending together into a low, consistent buzz. Victoria had been working nonstop for hours, the pressure of the competition weighing heavily on her shoulders. Every decision, every slice, every stir of her spoon felt like it carried the weight of the entire world.

But today, it wasn't just about the competition. The stinging critique from the celebrity chef still echoed in her mind, gnawing at her confidence. He had been right—her dish had lacked something vital, something raw and unpolished. She could feel the heat of his gaze lingering on her, as though he were waiting for her to reveal something deeper, something more than the technical expertise she was hiding behind.

The contestants were dismissed for the day, but Victoria lingered at her station, wiping down her workspace slowly, methodically. She couldn't afford to make another mistake. She had to prove herself—both to the judges and to the man who seemed to have pegged her from the moment she stepped onto this stage.

Out of the corner of her eye, she noticed him again. The celebrity chef was standing across the room, talking with one of the producers, his face a mask of concentration. But despite the distraction of his conversation, Victoria couldn't tear her eyes away from him. There was something about him—something magnetic—that pulled at her, a pull she couldn't resist.

A chill ran down her spine as she realized that she had already begun to study him in the same way he had studied her. The way he moved, the subtle shift in his posture when he was about to make a point. The tension in his jaw whenever he was displeased. It was all so deliberate, so calculated.

And yet, she knew very little about him. His public persona was polished, every word he spoke scripted, his life a series of well-curated moments. But she had seen enough in the brief exchanges they'd shared to know that there was more to him than the cameras allowed the world to see. The way his eyes had flickered when she presented her dish. The sharpness of his critique, not just of her cooking, but of her—her choices, her restraint.

A sudden voice broke her reverie, and she looked up to see one of the producers approaching her, a polite but insistent smile on his face. "Vera, can we have a quick word?" he asked, his tone neutral but firm.

Victoria nodded and followed him to the back of the kitchen, where the crew usually gathered between filming. The producer motioned for her to sit on a small bench near the door. As she did, she couldn't shake the feeling that something was off. The producer seemed too calm, too controlled for a conversation that should have been routine.

"Is everything alright?" she asked, her voice steady but her nerves beginning to edge their way to the surface.

The producer hesitated, his eyes darting around the room before meeting hers. "There's been some talk among the crew," he began, his voice lowering slightly. "About your performance. We're all aware that this is a high-stakes competition, but there's a question that's come up. One we need to address sooner rather than later."

Victoria's heart skipped a beat. She knew what was coming, but she didn't want to hear it. Not yet.

"What kind of question?" she asked, her voice just above a whisper, though she could already feel her pulse quickening.

"Some of the crew believe there's more to you than you're letting on," the producer said, his words carefully chosen. "There's been talk about your background, about who you really are."

Victoria stiffened. She knew she had been careful, too careful, but the walls were closing in. The last thing she wanted was for her identity to be exposed here, in front of the entire world. The anonymity she had fought so hard to maintain was beginning to slip away, and it terrified her.

"I don't know what you're talking about," she replied quickly, her voice tight.

"Vera," the producer said, his gaze piercing, "the truth is, we're not sure if you're just another contestant here, or if you're something else entirely. We've seen the way you handle yourself in the kitchen. You're too good to be just an ordinary cook. And then there's the fact that no one can seem to find any information on you, beyond what we've already been told."

Victoria's blood ran cold. How could they have figured it out so quickly? She had been so careful, hiding behind the mask of Vera Lee, keeping her true identity under wraps. But the producer wasn't done.

"We've also noticed the way you've been… reacting to the celebrity chef," he continued, leaning in slightly, as though making sure no one else could overhear. "The way you look at him. It's almost like you're trying to figure him out, the same way he's trying to figure you out."

Victoria's heart hammered in her chest. Was it that obvious? Had she been so transparent?

The producer gave her a small, knowing smile, though there was no warmth in it. "Listen, we don't want to cause any problems. But if there's something you're hiding, something we should know, now is the time to come clean. We can't protect you if it all comes crashing down in the middle of the competition. You need to make a decision. Who are you really?"

The words hung in the air like a threat. Victoria didn't respond immediately. Her mind was spinning, each thought crashing into the next in a dizzying whirlpool. She couldn't allow her secret to be revealed. Not here. Not now.

Taking a slow breath, she met the producer's eyes, her expression hardened. "I don't know what you think you know," she said, her voice cold and deliberate. "But I'm just a contestant here, trying to win. That's all there is to it."

The producer's smile faded slightly, but he didn't push further. "Alright, Vera," he said, his tone softening. "Just know that we're watching. Be careful. This competition is a lot more than just cooking."

Victoria stood, her heart still pounding in her chest. She felt the weight of his words pressing down on her, but she wasn't about to let anyone see how rattled she truly was. She had come too far to let something as trivial as a secret identity ruin everything.

As she turned to leave, her eyes caught a glimpse of him again—the celebrity chef, standing just beyond the door, his gaze locked onto hers with an intensity that made her skin prickle. There it was again, that knowing look, the one that made her feel like he could see right through her.

For a moment, she wondered if he had overheard the conversation. Was he onto her? Did he know who she really was?

Before she could even begin to question it, the celebrity chef took a step toward her, his movements slow but deliberate. The air between them grew charged, the space suddenly too small.

"I didn't mean to eavesdrop," he said, his voice low, almost teasing. "But I think we both know that secrets don't stay hidden for long in a place like this."

Victoria's breath caught in her throat. She had to say something, do something, but the words refused to come. Her mind was a maze of confusion, fear, and something else—something she couldn't name.

"You're playing a dangerous game, Vera," he continued, his tone now edged with something darker. "But I think I'll let you keep playing—for now. Just know that I'm watching."

With that, he turned and walked away, leaving Victoria standing there, her heart racing, her secret teetering on the edge of exposure. The game had changed. And she had no idea how much longer she could keep up the mask.

Five

A Recipe for Disaster

The kitchen was chaotic, a whirlwind of sounds and movement. Pots clanged against metal counters, knives sliced through ingredients, and the constant hum of the cameras added to the tension that hung in the air. Victoria's hands trembled slightly as she diced the carrots, her mind reeling from the conversation with the producer. The weight of his words still lingered in her chest like a dark cloud, but she couldn't afford to dwell on them now. The competition was far from over, and she had to stay focused.

But there was something else gnawing at her, something deeper than the stress of the competition itself. The celebrity chef had been watching her more closely than ever before, his eyes burning with an intensity that sent chills down her spine. It was like he knew she was hiding something. And worse, it seemed as though he was waiting for her to crack. To reveal herself.

She couldn't let that happen. Not now.

"Vera, you look like you've seen a ghost," came a voice from behind her.

Victoria turned, startled, to find one of the other contestants, a young man named Lucas, standing there with a wry smile on his face. He was young, ambitious, and had a tendency to push the limits in the kitchen. He wasn't the most experienced, but there was something about him—something that made him unpredictable. His presence in the kitchen always felt like a whirlwind, and in that moment, it was no different.

"I'm fine," she replied quickly, trying to mask the unease she felt. "Just focused."

Lucas raised an eyebrow, clearly not buying it. "Focus, huh? If you say so. But you've got the celebrity chef's eyes on you again. I'd say you've earned yourself a new kind of attention."

Victoria felt a cold shiver run down her spine. She tried to laugh it off, but the knot in her stomach tightened. "Just keeping my head down," she said, turning back to her station.

Lucas chuckled. "You're not fooling anyone, Vera. But if it makes you feel better, you're not the only one he's been watching closely. We all know what he's capable of, but you've got something he's interested in. That's what makes it fun, don't you think?"

Victoria forced a smile, but her mind was elsewhere. What did

Lucas mean by that? Was he implying that the celebrity chef was interested in her for something beyond her cooking? The thought sent a surge of anxiety through her veins. She couldn't afford to let anyone see her as anything other than just another contestant. Not here. Not now.

The sound of the timer ringing cut through her thoughts, signaling that the first round of the challenge was almost over. Her heart skipped a beat. She had to focus. She had to finish strong.

The challenge for this round was deceptively simple—make a dish using five mystery ingredients that would be judged on both creativity and execution. But what was simple in theory turned out to be a recipe for disaster.

Victoria's basket contained a few unripe peaches, a handful of mushrooms, a small cut of beef, a couple of potatoes, and a jar of pickled onions. On paper, they shouldn't have worked together. The challenge was to take those humble ingredients and transform them into something unexpected.

As she worked, her mind began to race. The chef's presence in the room was suffocating, his gaze following her every move like a hawk watching its prey. She could feel him watching her, not just for her skills, but for something more. There was an unnerving sensation that settled in her chest, one that told her he knew more than he was letting on.

With every chop of the knife, every toss of a pan, she couldn't shake the feeling that she was playing a game she might not be able to win. Her hands moved on autopilot, instinctively preparing the dish, but her thoughts kept drifting back to the moment with the producer. They had been talking about her, watching her. The mask she had so carefully constructed seemed to be slipping, and every second felt like it was pulling her closer to the edge.

The timer beeped again, signaling that the round was over. She stepped back, staring at her plate, trying to gather her thoughts. The dish was a mix of flavors and textures that didn't seem to make sense—caramelized peaches and earthy mushrooms, the beef cooked to perfection with a crispy crust, the sharpness of the pickled onions cutting through the sweetness of the fruit. It was unconventional, but it was her best attempt.

As she placed the dish on the judging table, she could feel the celebrity chef's eyes on her once more. His gaze didn't waver, his expression impassive, but there was a weight to his attention that made her skin crawl. She had to fight the urge to look away, to break the connection, but something about him kept drawing her in.

The judges began their critiques, their voices drowned out by the rush of blood in her ears. But then, the celebrity chef spoke, his voice cutting through the air like a blade.

"Vera," he said, his eyes never leaving hers, "this dish is… unexpected." He paused, taking a bite, his face unreadable. "But there's something wrong with it. The balance of flavors is off. The sweetness of the peaches and the bitterness of the mushrooms don't work together. The pickled onions are too overpowering for such a delicate dish."

Victoria's heart sank. The words stung, more than she had expected. She had hoped for something more—some recognition, some sign that her effort had paid off. But the chef's critique wasn't just harsh; it was personal. It felt like a direct attack, and she couldn't help but wonder if he was trying to break her.

"But…" the chef continued, his voice softening slightly, "there's potential here. You've got the skills, but you're holding back. You're too cautious, too afraid to truly commit."

His words cut deep, and she fought to keep her composure. She had been holding back, hadn't she? She had played it safe. But was it really the competition that had held her back? Or was it the weight of the mask she was wearing—the persona she had constructed to keep everyone at arm's length?

Victoria turned away, not wanting anyone to see the crack in her facade. The other judges spoke briefly, offering their thoughts, but she didn't hear them. All she could hear was the celebrity chef's voice, the challenge in his words, the subtle accusation in the air.

The round was over, and the contestants were ushered back to their stations. Victoria's hands were shaking as she cleaned her area, her thoughts swirling. The chef had been right about one thing—she was holding back. But why? What was stopping her from fully embracing the dish? The competition was about creativity, about pushing the boundaries of what food could be. So why had she played it so safe?

Her mind raced with the answer, and for the first time in weeks, she felt the weight of the truth settling over her like a heavy cloak. It wasn't the competition that had kept her from taking risks. It wasn't the fear of failure. No, it was something deeper, something that had been buried for far too long.

She wasn't just hiding her skills. She was hiding her identity. The person she had been before this competition—the woman who had built an empire from the ground up—wasn't the person she was now. Here, on this stage, she wasn't the heiress, the billionaire. She was Vera Lee, a woman who had nothing to lose. But in reality, she had everything to lose.

She was trapped in a game of her own making, and the celebrity chef—whether he knew it or not—was playing the same game. The challenge wasn't just about cooking anymore. It was about who she was. And the mask she had so carefully built was starting to crumble, piece by piece.

And the worst part? She had no idea if she could keep it up for much longer.

Six

The Heat is On

The room was alive with a nervous energy that buzzed like an electrical current. Contestants rushed around their stations, their movements swift and calculated, every second of time precious in the high-stakes kitchen. Victoria stood at her counter, her mind focused but her heart still pounding in her chest. She had only one goal: to survive.

The previous challenge had shaken her to her core. The harsh critique from the celebrity chef still echoed in her mind. He had said it, and it had struck deep into her soul: You're holding back. The words replayed over and over again, like a broken record. She had tried to hide behind a mask, tried to keep herself safe, but the celebrity chef saw right through her. He wasn't just critiquing her food; he was critiquing her—her reluctance to take risks, her fear of being exposed. It was a wake-up call, but one that she wasn't sure she was ready for.

"Alright, contestants!" The host's voice cut through the tension in the air. "We've got something special for you today. For this challenge, you will be preparing a dish that represents both your culinary style and your personal journey. You have one hour to create something that not only tastes incredible but tells a story."

Victoria's stomach flipped. A dish that represented her personal journey? Her life was a carefully constructed illusion, a fortress of secrets and carefully guarded identities. How was she supposed to prepare a dish that told the story of someone she wasn't?

The host continued, "You will be judged on creativity, presentation, and most importantly, your ability to show us who you truly are through your food."

Her heart rate accelerated. There it was again—the word that had haunted her from the start: who you truly are. It was as if the competition had become a metaphor for her own internal struggle. The longer she stayed here, the more she felt the pressure to reveal herself. To show them the person she was hiding from the world. But if she did that—if she allowed herself to be seen—it could all fall apart.

She couldn't let that happen. Not here. Not now.

The timer started, and the contestants scrambled to gather their ingredients, the sound of their frantic movements mixing with the rising tension in the room. Victoria's mind raced. She needed something that would wow the judges, something that would make them see her culinary skill, but also something that would allow her to stay hidden. Something that felt personal but still kept her true identity a secret.

Her hands moved automatically as she began to gather ingredients. She scanned the table in front of her, eyes flicking from one item to the next: a handful of herbs, some vegetables, and a small portion of chicken. The challenge had given her a wide range of ingredients to work with, but it also forced her to confront something she wasn't prepared for. She had to make a dish that represented who she was without revealing who she was. The question that loomed over her now wasn't just about flavor—it was about identity.

Victoria's fingers brushed against the chicken, and a wave of clarity washed over her. She couldn't go through with this challenge by hiding behind the veil of Vera Lee anymore. She needed to confront the dish head-on, raw and unafraid, and trust in her own abilities. But she couldn't reveal her true self— not yet. Not until she was ready.

She moved quickly, focusing on the task at hand, even as the pressure mounted around her. The celebrity chef's eyes were on her again, his presence like a shadow hanging over her every move. He had been more present in this competition than she had anticipated. His piercing gaze followed her, scrutinizing her every action, like a hawk circling its prey. His challenge still haunted her—You're holding back. And now, with this dish, it felt like the moment of truth was finally here.

As she began to prepare the chicken, slicing it into perfect strips and seasoning it with the herbs, Victoria felt the heat of the competition intensify. She was no longer just competing with the other contestants. She was competing with herself— fighting to stay hidden while simultaneously trying to push past the walls she had so carefully built around her.

The celebrity chef stepped closer to her station, his eyes never leaving her. The other contestants seemed to notice, their movements slowing as they realized what was happening. His presence was almost suffocating, like the air had thickened around her.

"Vera," he said, his voice low, just loud enough for her to hear, "you've got the ingredients. Now let's see if you've got the courage to make something extraordinary."

His words sent a shiver through her. It wasn't just a challenge to her culinary skills; it was a challenge to everything she had built. His tone was probing, like he was daring her to show him something deeper, something more than the carefully controlled exterior she had constructed.

Her heart raced, but she didn't look up. She kept her focus on the chicken, her hands moving faster now, her movements precise as she worked with an almost mechanical determination. She couldn't afford to get distracted by him. She had to finish this dish. And she had to do it in a way that kept her secret safe.

"Twenty minutes remaining!" the host called out, snapping her back to reality. Victoria had already started cooking the chicken in a sizzling pan, the smell of herbs and seasoning wafting through the air. She needed to focus on bringing the dish together, something that would speak to the judges without speaking too loudly. She couldn't afford to make any mistakes now.

As the seconds ticked away, the pressure began to build. The other contestants were moving with increasing urgency, the frantic energy in the room growing more intense with each passing minute. But for Victoria, it was a slow burn, every minute stretching into what felt like hours. She was still thinking about the challenge that lay ahead, the moment when she would have to serve her dish and face the inevitable judgment of the celebrity chef.

She glanced up for a split second, and there he was—standing just beyond her station, his eyes fixed on her as if waiting for her to slip up. His gaze was intense, focused, and Victoria could feel the weight of his scrutiny pressing on her like a physical force.

Her fingers tightened around the knife as she sliced through the vegetables, the sharp sound cutting through the tension in the room. Her mind flashed back to the words he had said to her: You're holding back. It was as if those words had become a mantra in her mind, a constant reminder that she needed to do more, to be more. She couldn't keep playing it safe, not if she wanted to win. Not if she wanted to prove that she was more than just a name.

The timer rang again, and Victoria's heart skipped a beat. The dish was nearly done. She had made her final touches, a delicate arrangement of roasted vegetables alongside the perfectly cooked chicken, garnished with a sprig of fresh herbs. It was simple, but it had depth. She hoped it was enough.

As she approached the judging table, she felt the full weight of the moment. The celebrity chef was watching her closely, his expression unreadable. The other judges were equally silent, their eyes fixed on her dish. Her stomach twisted in knots. This was it. This was the moment where everything could either fall into place or fall apart.

She set the dish down in front of them, stepping back as the judges began to examine it. The celebrity chef didn't speak at first. He simply took a bite, his eyes narrowing slightly as he tasted it. The silence was unbearable. It felt like the entire room was holding its breath, waiting for his verdict. Victoria's heart thudded in her chest as she watched him carefully, searching for any sign of approval or disapproval. But his face remained a mask, and the silence stretched on.

Finally, he spoke, his voice steady and calm. "This dish..." he began, pausing as he continued to taste it. "This dish is exactly what I was hoping to see. It's simple, but there's something about it. It's balanced, it's flavorful, and it's true to what you're capable of." He looked up at her, his eyes locking with hers. "Finally, you're not holding back."

Victoria's breath caught in her throat. She hadn't expected that. The challenge had been one of the hardest moments she'd faced so far, and yet here she was—having finally stepped beyond the mask she'd been hiding behind.

But as the words sunk in, a new weight settled in her chest. She had shown them who she truly was. But what did that mean for her future in this competition? What would happen now that she had let down her guard?

Seven

Secrets Unveiled

The kitchen was almost unnaturally quiet, the usual hum of activity replaced by a heavy stillness that seemed to seep into every corner of the room. Victoria's mind raced, her heart pounding as she moved slowly between her station and the prep counter, her hands betraying the tension that gripped her chest. She had done it—she had finally stopped holding back. The celebrity chef's words, though unspoken at first, had cut through the facade she had spent weeks building. The mask was slipping, and she wasn't sure if she was ready to face the consequences.

It had been an hour since the challenge ended, and the judges had dismissed the contestants for a break. But Victoria couldn't rest—not with the burning sensation in her chest. Not when she could feel the heat of the celebrity chef's gaze on her from across the room.

She glanced up. There he was, his broad shoulders and sharp features making him a commanding presence, even from a distance. He stood alone, his hands in his pockets, staring into space as if lost in thought. The same look he always wore, a mask of calculated indifference. But there was something different now. He wasn't just watching her as he had before. It was deeper this time, more intense, like he was waiting for something—waiting for her.

Victoria forced herself to look away. She couldn't let him get under her skin. But the truth was, he already had.

It wasn't just the competition anymore. It wasn't about her food or her technique or even about the prize. It was about the fact that the celebrity chef had seen through her. He had seen past the carefully constructed image she had worked so hard to build, the false identity she had cloaked herself in to protect her real self. He had recognized her for who she truly was.

And now she had no idea what to do with that truth.

As she moved across the kitchen to grab a drink of water, she felt his eyes on her once again. She knew he was watching her. It was almost unbearable. She could feel the weight of his gaze like an invisible force pressing against her chest, suffocating her. She took a deep breath, trying to steady herself, trying to focus on the task ahead, but the question that had been haunting her for the past few days kept nagging at her: What if he's right?

The sound of footsteps interrupted her thoughts, and she turned to find Lucas, the ambitious young contestant, walking toward her. His smile was wide, almost too wide, like he had something to say, but wasn't sure how to say it. She sighed inwardly. Lucas had always been a bit too eager, too quick to jump into everyone's business.

"You did it," he said, his voice low but carrying the unmistakable hint of intrigue. "I thought you'd never stop holding back. But you did. That dish… it was good. No, better than good. It was you."

Victoria narrowed her eyes, a small flicker of irritation sparking within her. "What do you mean by that?"

Lucas shrugged, his grin never wavering. "I mean, you stopped pretending to be something you're not. Everyone could see it. Even the celebrity chef. And you know what? He noticed. More than anyone else here. And he respects you for it."

Victoria's stomach twisted. She didn't need Lucas to tell her what the celebrity chef was thinking. The way he had looked at her during the critique, the way his eyes had softened ever so slightly when he spoke—it wasn't just about the dish anymore. She was no longer just another contestant. She had caught his attention. And now, it felt like she was walking a tightrope, with no safety net below.

"I didn't come here for his respect," Victoria muttered, her voice barely above a whisper. "I came here to win."

Lucas tilted his head, his grin turning sly. "I think you've already won, Vera. You've won more than just the competition. You've won his attention. That's what this is all about, isn't it?"

Victoria froze, her heart hammering in her chest. "What are you talking about?" Her voice cracked slightly despite her attempt to stay composed.

"Come on," Lucas said, his tone lowering to a conspiratorial whisper. "Everyone's talking about it. There's something between you two. It's not just about food. It's… personal. The way he watches you when you cook. The way he challenges you. It's more than just a competition for him. And it's more than just a cooking show for you."

Victoria's breath caught in her throat. Her instincts screamed at her to shut him down, to deny it, to walk away. But the words wouldn't come. She felt as though she were suffocating under the weight of what Lucas had just implied.

"No," she said finally, forcing the words out through clenched teeth. "There's nothing between us."

But even as she said it, she felt the lie slip out of her mouth, hollow and unconvincing. Because in the silence that followed, she couldn't deny what Lucas had said. There was something between her and the celebrity chef. Something unspoken. Something that had been building since the moment they had met.

As she turned away from Lucas, her mind spun, her thoughts racing in a whirlwind of confusion and fear. She had thought she could control this—thought she could stay hidden behind the mask of Vera Lee. But the longer she stayed, the more it felt like the mask was slipping, and she was powerless to stop it.

Her heart pounded as she returned to her station, trying to shake off the heavy feeling of vulnerability that had crept in. But as she approached her counter, she saw him—standing just a few feet away, his presence like a physical weight in the room. The celebrity chef.

He hadn't spoken a word to her since the challenge, but there he was, watching her with that same, unreadable look in his eyes. He didn't approach her immediately. Instead, he just stood there, observing, as if waiting for something—waiting for her to make the first move.

Victoria's pulse quickened. She knew he was aware of the way she felt, the way the competition had changed everything for her. She could feel the tension in the air, thick and heavy, as if the space between them was charged with electricity. And then, after what felt like an eternity, he took a step forward.

"Vera," he said, his voice low and steady, "we need to talk."

Her breath caught in her throat. She had known this moment was coming. She had known that the truth couldn't stay hidden forever. But that didn't mean she was ready for it.

"I'm not interested in talking," she replied, her voice sharp, defensive. "I just want to finish the competition."

The celebrity chef didn't flinch. He didn't retreat. Instead, he took another step forward, closing the distance between them. "It's not just about winning, is it?" he said quietly. "It's never been just about food for you."

Victoria froze. She couldn't breathe. He had said it. He had finally said what she had been too afraid to admit to herself.

He reached out, his hand hovering just inches from her arm. "You're not just here to prove your skills, Vera. You're here to prove something to yourself. You're here to find something that's been missing. But you can't keep hiding behind this mask forever."

Her pulse hammered in her ears. She wanted to say something, anything, but her throat felt dry, her words caught in her chest.

"I'm not who you think I am," she whispered, the words slipping out before she could stop them.

For a moment, the celebrity chef didn't respond. He simply studied her, his eyes softening ever so slightly. It was almost as if he knew. As if he had already figured it out.

"I know who you are, Vera," he said softly. "And I know what you're afraid of. But running from it won't make it go away."

Victoria felt as though the world had shifted beneath her feet. The truth was out there, hanging between them, and she had nowhere to hide.

"I can't do this anymore," she muttered, her voice breaking.

He stepped back, giving her space, but his eyes never left her. "Then don't. Don't hide. Don't run. Be who you are. You might be surprised at what you find."

With that, he turned and walked away, leaving her standing there, her heart in her throat, the weight of the secret she had been holding for so long finally threatening to overwhelm her.

The game had changed. The mask was slipping—and there was no going back.

Eight

Heart Over Recipe

The hours that followed the conversation with the celebrity chef felt like an eternity. Victoria barely registered the passage of time, her mind caught in an endless loop of thoughts that refused to settle. The words he had said to her, the way he had looked at her, were etched in her mind like a brand. It wasn't just about cooking anymore. It wasn't about winning the competition. It was about something deeper, something terrifying that she hadn't been ready to face.

"I know who you are, Vera," his voice echoed in her mind. "And I know what you're afraid of. But running from it won't make it go away."

She had always believed that she could hide behind the veil of her carefully constructed identity. She had convinced herself that the persona of Vera Lee was enough to shield her from everything—her past, her fears, her insecurities. But now, everything was unraveling. The celebrity chef had seen through her. He had seen through the mask she had spent years building, and in doing so, he had exposed something she wasn't ready to confront.

As the competition continued, it became increasingly difficult for her to maintain the distance she had once prided herself on. The other contestants were growing more and more focused on their own dishes, but for Victoria, the battle was no longer in the kitchen. The true struggle was internal, a war between the woman she had pretended to be and the woman she had buried deep inside.

The celebrity chef's presence loomed over her, like a shadow she couldn't escape. She had tried to block him out, to focus on the task at hand, but his gaze was always there, watching her. He was waiting, waiting for her to make the first move, waiting for her to step forward and confront the truth of who she was.

The clock on the wall ticked away, the seconds slipping through her fingers like sand. She glanced around the room, taking in the faces of her fellow competitors, each of them focused on their own work. The pressure of the competition had reached its peak, and the air was thick with tension. But it was the celebrity chef who dominated her thoughts. His eyes, the way he had looked at her, the way he had pierced through her carefully constructed walls—it was all she could think about.

Victoria's hands moved mechanically as she prepared for the next challenge, her mind elsewhere. The ingredients in front of her seemed foreign, detached, as if she were on autopilot. She wasn't thinking about the dish, the flavors, or the technique. She was thinking about what had been revealed. About the truth that was slowly, painfully, coming to the surface.

"Ten minutes left!" the host's voice rang out, pulling her from her thoughts. The others around her were already deep in their work, moving with purpose. But Victoria stood still, her heart pounding, her hands trembling. She couldn't seem to focus. Her mind was filled with images of the celebrity chef's face, his eyes, his voice. The way he had challenged her to stop hiding.

Her thoughts were interrupted by a soft knock at her station. She turned to find him standing there, the celebrity chef, his expression unreadable. Her breath caught in her throat as he looked at her with those piercing eyes.

"We need to talk," he said quietly, his voice low but firm.

Victoria's stomach dropped. She wasn't sure what to expect, but she knew it wasn't going to be easy. She had been running from this moment, avoiding it, but now it was here. She had no choice but to face it.

She nodded wordlessly, setting down the knife she had been holding. The tension in the room seemed to amplify as they stepped away from the others, moving toward the back of the kitchen where they could speak privately. Victoria's pulse raced, her mind whirling with every possible scenario. What would he say? What would happen now?

They stood in silence for a moment, the weight of the conversation hanging between them. Victoria tried to steady her breath, to calm her nerves, but nothing seemed to work. She felt like she was on the edge of something she couldn't control, and the closer she got to the truth, the more terrified she became.

"Vera," he began, his voice quiet but carrying an intensity that made her heart race. "You've been running from yourself. From the truth of who you are. But you don't have to keep pretending."

Victoria swallowed hard, her throat dry. "I'm not pretending," she said, but even as the words left her mouth, she knew they weren't true. She had been pretending for so long that she didn't even remember who she really was anymore.

"Stop lying to yourself," he said softly, his eyes searching hers. "You've been hiding behind this mask, behind the idea of who you think you should be. But who you are is so much more than that. You can't keep running from it."

Victoria felt a knot form in her stomach. She had never been good at facing the truth, especially when it was this raw, this exposed. But the longer she stood there, the more she realized that the truth was undeniable. The celebrity chef had seen her. Not the persona, not the carefully crafted image, but the person beneath it all. And in doing so, he had pulled something from her that she wasn't ready to confront.

"I can't," she whispered, her voice barely audible. "I can't let anyone see me. Not like that."

The celebrity chef's gaze softened, and for a brief moment, he didn't look like the intense, intimidating figure she had always seen him as. He looked… human. Vulnerable, even. "You don't have to do this alone, Vera," he said, his voice low, but carrying an undeniable warmth. "You don't have to be afraid anymore. You're not the only one who's been hiding."

His words hit her like a wave, crashing over her with a force that left her breathless. For the first time in the competition, she realized that he wasn't just talking about her. He was talking about himself.

She blinked, trying to process what he had just said. "What do you mean?" she asked, her voice barely above a whisper.

He hesitated for a moment before speaking again. "I've spent my life hiding behind my success. Hiding behind the persona of the celebrity chef. The truth is, I've never let anyone get close enough to see who I really am. And maybe that's why I pushed you so hard. Because I saw something in you—something real— and I was afraid of it. Afraid of what it would mean if I let you in."

Victoria stared at him, her heart racing in her chest. She hadn't expected this. She hadn't expected him to open up to her, to reveal something so raw, so vulnerable. It caught her off guard, and for a moment, she didn't know what to say.

But then, slowly, something inside her shifted. She could feel the walls she had built around herself beginning to crumble. He was right. She had been hiding. Hiding from the truth, hiding from the person she really was. And maybe, just maybe, it was time to stop running.

"I'm scared," she said, her voice barely audible. "I'm scared of what will happen if I let go of the mask. If I let people see who I really am."

The celebrity chef took a step closer, his eyes never leaving hers. "You don't have to be scared," he said softly. "Because who you are is enough. And it always has been."

The words hung in the air between them, a promise, a truth that neither of them had been ready to face until now. Victoria's heart beat loudly in her chest as she realized something profound. She wasn't just fighting for a win in the competition. She was fighting for something deeper. Something that could change everything.

And in that moment, she knew that the game had changed. The competition wasn't just about food anymore. It was about heart. It was about facing the truth, no matter how terrifying it might be.

For the first time since she had entered this competition, Victoria felt a sense of clarity. She wasn't alone in this fight. And maybe, just maybe, she didn't have to hide anymore.

With a deep breath, she nodded. "I'm ready," she whispered, her voice strong despite the fear that still lingered in her chest.

The celebrity chef gave her a small, almost imperceptible smile, his eyes softening with something that looked like respect. "Good," he said. "Now, let's see what you can really do."

And with that, the challenge was no longer about winning. It was about being seen. Truly seen. And for the first time, Victoria was ready to face it.

Nine

The Final Showdown

The morning of the final challenge arrived with an ominous stillness that settled over the kitchen. The usual chaos and frantic energy of the previous rounds had given way to a tense silence, thick with anticipation. The cameras, the crew, and the lights were all in place, but today, it felt different. It felt like the calm before a storm.

Victoria stood at her station, her hands wrapped around the cool handle of her knife, staring down at the ingredients in front of her. The challenge was simple in theory: prepare a three-course meal that would showcase everything she had learned, everything she was capable of. But the weight of the task was crushing, the pressure of the final round pushing her to the edge.

She had made it this far, and yet it felt like the hardest part of the competition had only just begun. The previous rounds had been a test of skill, of technique, but this—this was about more than that. This was the final test. It was about showing who she truly was, about standing in front of the judges and facing not just the competition but herself.

The celebrity chef's words echoed in her mind: Who you are is enough. And it always has been. She had spent so long hiding, so long pretending to be someone she wasn't, but now there was no more room for pretending. It wasn't just about the dish she was going to create. It was about letting the world see the real her—the woman behind the mask.

But that was the part that terrified her the most. The thought of being exposed, of revealing everything she had worked so hard to hide. The thought of letting the celebrity chef, of all people, see her as she truly was.

The timer started, the harsh sound slicing through the stillness of the room, and Victoria snapped out of her reverie. There was no time to think about fear now. She had one hour. Sixty minutes to make a statement, to leave her mark on this competition. She had to focus. She had to push past the fear, past the self-doubt, and just create.

Her hands moved instinctively as she reached for the ingredients. The basket in front of her was full of familiar items—fresh herbs, vegetables, a small cut of lamb, some delicate seafood, and a few surprises hidden at the bottom. It was a diverse range of ingredients, but there was one constant in her mind: this dish needed to tell a story. Not just any story. Her story.

She glanced up, taking in the other contestants. They were focused, each one working in their own world, but there was an undercurrent of competition in the air. The final round always brought out the best—and the worst—in people. The tension was palpable, but no one seemed more on edge than Victoria. She could feel the weight of the eyes on her—the cameras, the producers, and, most of all, the celebrity chef. He was there, always there, watching, waiting. His gaze never strayed from her, and it made her uneasy.

She could sense the other contestants' curiosity, too. The rumors had already started circulating about her. The whispers about her real identity, about what she was hiding, had spread like wildfire. The producers had warned her, and Lucas had mentioned it too. Everyone could see it—the way she moved, the way she cooked. She wasn't just another contestant. She was something more. Something that made them nervous.

And that was exactly why she couldn't falter. She couldn't let them see her stumble. Not now. Not when she was so close to the finish line.

The lamb in front of her was perfect—tender, marbled with fat, and ready to be seared. She moved quickly, slicing through the vegetables with precision, the knife gliding effortlessly through the fresh produce. She seared the lamb in a hot pan, the sizzle filling the kitchen as the fat began to render. The smell was intoxicating. She let the lamb rest, the juices pooling in the pan as she prepared to move on to the next dish.

The next dish. The seafood. The pressure mounted as she

realized that she wasn't just cooking for the judges anymore. She was cooking for herself. She had come this far, and she knew it wouldn't matter how good her dishes were if she wasn't willing to give everything.

The clock ticked down, each second slipping away as Victoria's hands flew over the ingredients. The delicate balance of flavors had to be perfect. The lamb had to be cooked to the right temperature—medium-rare, the crust crispy but not burned. The seafood had to be fresh, lightly seasoned, the texture tender but firm. Everything had to be flawless.

She was lost in her work, her focus absolute, when she felt a presence behind her. She turned, startled, to find the celebrity chef standing just a few feet away, watching her with that same, inscrutable expression. His eyes were intense, studying her every move.

"Need any help?" he asked, his tone casual, but there was an underlying edge to it.

Victoria swallowed hard. She had heard the rumors, heard the stories about how he could manipulate contestants, how he could break them down to get what he wanted. But she had no intention of letting him do that to her. Not today.

"I'm fine," she said, her voice firm. "I've got this."

The celebrity chef nodded, but there was something in the way he looked at her that sent a chill down her spine. "Good. Because if you can't handle the pressure now, you'll never be able to handle what's coming."

Victoria clenched her jaw. What was he playing at? She had no intention of backing down, no matter how much he pushed her.

"I can handle it," she said, meeting his gaze with defiance.

He studied her for a moment longer, then, as if satisfied, turned away and walked back to his station. The tension remained, hanging between them like a storm cloud, but Victoria refused to let it break her. She had a job to do.

The final dish was coming together. Her hands moved with confidence now, the steps of the recipe as familiar as breathing. She could see the end result in her mind's eye—perfectly seared lamb, a vibrant medley of vegetables, delicate seafood, and a sauce that would bring it all together. Every element was in place, but there was one final touch she needed—something that would elevate the dish, something that would make it her own.

The seconds ticked away, and with each passing moment, Victoria's heart rate quickened. There was no time for mistakes. No time to second-guess herself. This was her moment. This was her chance to show the judges who she truly was—not just as a chef, but as a person.

"Five minutes!" the host called out, and the urgency in his voice spurred her into action.

Victoria's hands moved faster, her focus razor-sharp. She plated the lamb first, carefully arranging the vegetables and seafood around it. The sauce went on last, drizzled delicately over the entire dish. It was simple, elegant, and yet it carried a depth of flavor that would speak volumes.

She stepped back, surveying her creation. It wasn't just food. It was a reflection of who she had become over the course of the competition. It was a reflection of the risks she had taken, the walls she had broken down, and the truth she had finally embraced.

The final seconds of the challenge ticked away, and as the timer rang, signaling the end, Victoria felt a strange sense of calm wash over her. She had done it. She had faced the pressure, faced the fear, and created something beautiful.

The celebrity chef's eyes flickered to her dish as she set it down in front of the judges. He said nothing, but she could see the small nod of approval. He had been watching her every move, and now, she had finally shown him what she was capable of.

As the judges began to taste the dishes, the room fell into a tense silence. Victoria stood back, her hands trembling, but her heart steady. This was it. There was no going back now.

The celebrity chef took a bite of her dish, his eyes narrowing slightly as he chewed. He swallowed, then took another bite. The silence stretched on, the tension unbearable.

Finally, he spoke. "This is the dish I've been waiting for," he said, his voice low but clear. "It's balanced. It's daring. And most importantly, it's you. This is what happens when you stop hiding."

Victoria's heart soared. The judges began to murmur their approval, but it was his words that she held onto. *This is you.*

The game was over. The competition was done. But for Victoria, the real victory had been in showing the world—and herself—who she truly was.

She had stepped out from behind the mask. And now, there was no turning back.

Ten

A New Beginning

The final bell rang, its echo bouncing off the walls of the kitchen, signaling the end of the competition. The silence that followed was deafening, as though the world had frozen in place. The cameras had stopped rolling, the lights dimmed, and the bustling hum of the crew quieted to a mere whisper in the background. For Victoria, it felt as though time itself had suspended, leaving her suspended in the moment. She had done it. She had shown them everything— her skill, her creativity, her heart. But as the seconds ticked by, her chest tightened with a strange unease.

The judges were still seated, their expressions unreadable, their faces obscured behind the masks of professionalism. The celebrity chef sat at the head of the table, his piercing gaze fixed on her plate, his lips pressed together in a tight line. His silence was both an affirmation and a challenge. She had spent so long trying to decipher his every word, trying to figure out what he truly thought, but now, in this moment, she realized something. It didn't matter what he thought anymore. She had already won.

But winning wasn't the same as overcoming her own fears.

Victoria stood by her station, her heart pounding in her chest as she waited for the judges to deliberate. The faces of the other contestants blurred in her peripheral vision. She wasn't focused on them. She wasn't focused on anything except the gnawing sensation in her stomach, the worry that clung to her every thought. What if the judges didn't see what she had seen? What if, in the end, the truth she had finally embraced was nothing more than a fleeting illusion?

She glanced over at the celebrity chef. He was still silent, his gaze unwavering as he examined her dish. His expression hadn't changed. She had given him everything she had, but what if it wasn't enough? What if the mask she had worn for so long was the very thing he had wanted to see destroyed, and by doing so, she had lost everything that mattered?

The host's voice cut through the tension, bringing her back to reality. "We've reached the end of the competition," the host announced. "The judges have made their final decision. Now, it's time for the verdict."

Victoria's heart stopped. The world around her seemed to slow, each word from the host hanging in the air like a weight she couldn't escape. Her palms were slick with sweat, her breath shallow as she stood frozen, waiting for what felt like an eternity.

Finally, the celebrity chef spoke, his voice calm but with an unmistakable edge to it. "This has been a competition unlike any other. From the start, you've all shown skill, creativity, and an incredible work ethic. But in the end, only one can emerge as the winner. And that winner is the person who can take the pressure, who can show us not just technique, but who they truly are."

Victoria's heart raced in her chest. She could feel the weight of his words bearing down on her, the quiet challenge in his tone reminding her of everything she had gone through. The competition had never been about cooking alone. It had been about revealing who she was beneath the surface, about stripping away the layers and exposing the truth.

He paused for a moment, letting the silence stretch between them. Victoria's pulse thudded in her ears, drowning out everything else. She had stopped hiding. She had let the world see her. Had she made the right choice?

"The winner," he continued, his voice lowering, "is someone who has not only shown exceptional culinary skill but has also demonstrated courage, vulnerability, and authenticity. Someone who has stopped hiding and embraced who they truly are."

Victoria held her breath, her hands trembling at her sides. The words felt like a punch in the stomach, but in a way that didn't hurt. It was the kind of punch that lifted her up, that made her realize how far she had come.

"And that person," the celebrity chef finished, his gaze locking with hers, "is you, Vera."

The world seemed to shatter around her. It was as though everything stopped, her body going numb as the words sunk in. She had won. But more than that, she had finally been seen. Not as a contestant, not as the woman behind the mask, but as herself.

The applause that followed was a distant hum in her ears. She could hear the cheers, the excited chatter from the other contestants, but it all felt so far away. In that moment, there was only her and him. The celebrity chef stood, his expression softening just slightly. For the first time, he looked at her not with scrutiny, not with that piercing intensity, but with something closer to respect.

Victoria took a step forward, her legs unsteady as she tried to process the reality of what had just happened. She had come into this competition afraid, uncertain of who she was, unsure of what she could offer the world. But now, standing before the man who had pushed her to her breaking point and beyond, she realized that this wasn't just about winning a cooking competition. It was about finding herself.

"Thank you," she whispered, the words coming out hoarse, as if she hadn't spoken in days. "Thank you for seeing me. For seeing the real me."

The celebrity chef nodded, his expression softening for the briefest of moments. "I didn't just see you, Vera," he said quietly. "I saw what you were hiding. And I'm proud of you for letting it out."

Victoria's chest tightened, her emotions threatening to spill over. She had thought that the hardest part of this journey would be creating a dish that impressed the judges. But in truth, the hardest part had been creating the person she had become. The person she was always meant to be.

As the host moved forward, offering congratulations and a trophy, Victoria's eyes drifted toward the other contestants. They were smiling, clapping, but beneath their smiles, she could see the unspoken recognition—the acknowledgment of her strength, her growth. She hadn't just won the title of "Ultimate Chef." She had won something far more valuable. She had won herself.

The trophy felt heavy in her hands, but not in a burdensome way. It felt like a symbol of everything she had overcome, every fear she had faced, every secret she had let go of. It was a tangible representation of her journey—a journey that had started with a disguise and ended with the revelation of who she truly was.

"Thank you," she said again, her voice gaining strength as she spoke. "Thank you to everyone who believed in me. But more importantly, thank you to myself—for not giving up. For not staying hidden."

The celebrity chef stepped closer, offering a smile that was softer than anything she had ever expected from him. "You've earned this, Vera," he said. "And more. You're not just a chef. You're someone who has the courage to be real. And that's something the world needs."

Victoria's chest swelled with pride as she held the trophy aloft, the weight of it no longer an anchor but a beacon. She had done it. She had faced her fears, faced the person she had been hiding from for so long, and now, she was free.

The lights in the studio seemed brighter now, the cameras less intrusive. The world around her felt alive in a way it never had before. The celebrity chef stepped back, his presence still lingering, but now, there was no tension. There was no challenge. There was only the mutual respect between them.

As the applause continued, Victoria felt something shift inside her. The mask had finally fallen, and in its place was a woman who was no longer afraid to be herself. And for the first time in her life, she understood what it meant to be truly free.

This wasn't the end of her journey. It was just the beginning. A new beginning. One where she could finally be the person she was always meant to be—bold, unapologetic, and unafraid to step into the light.

She had won. But more than that, she had found her true self. And that was the greatest victory of all.